"Warm, vital and human... will be of interest not only to seminarians, but to priests and lay people as well."
— Elisabeth Murphy Nydegger

"Engaging and direct. Gives a new ring to seminary teachings."
— *The Ensign*

"Catherine was a spiritual mother, with a vast experience of the spiritual life. In *Dear Seminarian,* she addresses a wide range of topics germane to priestly and spiritual formation. She received as spiritual sons, those who sought her guidance. Catherine's starting point was always priestly identity—the priest extends the incarnation of Christ in history; he is an icon of Christ, or 'another Christ.' She sought to prepare them to shepherd God's people in the spiritual crisis and challenge facing the 20th century, a crisis that has continued and deepened in the present."
— Father Don Guglielmi, in *Staritsa: The Spiritual Maternity of Catherine Doherty*

"The message of *Dear Seminarian* is, in my opinion, even more pertinent today than when it was first published.... With the passing of time Catherine Doherty may become appreciated as a profound spiritual director."
— Bishop Paul V. Dudley
Bishop Emeritus of Sioux Falls, SD

"I feel confident that *Dear Seminarian* will prove a friendly and helpful guide to young men on their way up the steps of God's altar... There is doubtfully any woman who has spoken oftener in seminaries to future priests over the whole American continent than Catherine Doherty."
— Bishop William J. Smith,
former Bishop of Pembroke, ON

"Provocative reading for priests and lay people alike."
— *The Catholic Transcript*

dear seminarian

Letters from a lay apostle
on becoming a shepherd of souls.

Catherine de Hueck Doherty

Madonna House Publications
Combermere, Ontario, Canada

Nihil Obstat: Charles J. Jones, V.F., *Censor Deputatus*, March 15, 1950.

Imprimatur: William Joseph Smith, Bishop of Pembroke, March 25, 1950.

Madonna House Publications®
2888 Dafoe Rd, RR 2
Combermere ON K0J 1L0

www.madonnahouse.org/publications

Dear Seminarian
by Catherine de Hueck Doherty (née Kolyschkine)
© 2003 Madonna House Publications. All rights reserved.

New Revised Third Edition

Second printing, March 10, 2009

Printed in Canada

Edited by Marian Heiberger

Design by Rob Huston
This book is set in Minion, with display lines in TradeGothic.

National Library of Canada Cataloguing in Publication

Doherty, Catherine de Hueck, 1896–1985
  Dear seminarian / Catherine Doherty. — New rev. ed.

ISBN 978-0-921440-85-7

  1. Pastoral theology—Catholic Church. 2. Catholic Church—Clergy—Office. I. Title.

BX903.D64 2003   253   C2003-906080-2

To

the Most Rev. William J. Smith

and his successor

the Most Rev. Joseph R. Windle,

Bishops of Pembroke

About this revision

Catherine wrote the first edition of *Dear Seminarian* in 1950, based on her pioneer experience in the lay apostolate up until that time, known as Friendship House. In this revision, the material that was time-specific has been replaced by selections from her more recent talks and writings. We have tried to remain faithful to her basic intent throughout the book.

— Editor

Contents

1 | Your awesome calling

"Through Ordination, you receive...the Spirit of Christ, who makes you like him, so that you can act in his name and so that his very mind and heart might live in you."

— *Pope John Paul II, homily to 5000 priests, October 9th, 1984*

Dear seminarian, I have been praying for you with all my heart, for you may be one of our future priests, and priests are a miracle of God's love for us. A man, through the sacrament of Ordination, becomes another Christ, with powers that go beyond human imagination.

It may seem strange to you that a laywoman should want to discuss with you this infinite, this awesome, this almost miraculous vocation of the priesthood. The more so that you are already on your way to it, and presumably know more than I ever shall of its beauty, its dignity, its sacrifice, its joys and sorrows, and its glorious final end. Yet humbly and respectfully, I still want to talk with you about being a priest.

For I—a laywoman and a pioneer in the 'lay apostolate'—have, from the age of twelve, offered my life for priests. I love priests intensely. Many hundreds of priests have come for spiritual renewal to Madonna House (the apostolate and community of lay men, lay women, and priests which I founded), and by the grace of God have been strengthened in their vocation; various priests have even returned to active ministry in their stupendous vocation.

In my vigils at night, and in my prayers during the day, I had a desire to do something for future priests. This little book was written in response to numerous letters and visits I received from seminarians, asking advice about the priesthood and about formation for this awesome calling. We lay people—for whom the priesthood exists because priests are ordained for us—must do everything in our power to foster that vocation.

When a man feels called to become a priest, that means God has put his hand on his shoulder and said, "Come, follow me." And he follows. What a tremendous thing to see a fellow human being who obviously, courageously states that he is a follower of Christ. Christ says, "I have chosen you; you have not chosen me."

Tomorrow or the day after you will become a priest. I dwell on that day of days, because to me it is indeed the most stupendous day given any man—the day when one of us, an ordinary, mere creature, becomes another Christ—*alter Christus*—providing us, his flock, with the life-giving sacraments; teaching us his infinite truths; leading us on the paths of his love to life everlasting. I must tell you that it has always been very hard for me to attend an ordination because the awesomeness and majesty, both of God and of the proceedings, overwhelm me. If one really understands what is going on at an ordination, one should faint, even if he or she be strong, because a miracle takes place, beyond all proportions.

A priest has the power of healing bodies, of healing souls, of bringing back the prodigal son. He has the power of feeding the hungry: those who haven't bread and those who have, for the Bread that the priest gives assuages the hunger of both poor and rich. The enormity of God's love for us never dawns on us.

Christ loved us so passionately, so foolishly, so beyond all bounds of love that we can experience, that he left us himself in his priests. He takes a sinner, just like ourselves, and through a special anointing and the laying on of hands by a bishop, the man is impregnated, impenetrated, filled with Jesus Christ. Here is God descending into a sinner, and not only descending, but filling that man with himself.

Into these men he has entered, not like milk enters a pitcher, or tea goes into a cup. No. He has become the cup, as well as entered into the cup. Priests really become another Christ. It is the hands of Christ that anoint. It is the lips of Christ that pronounce the words that change the bread and wine into his Body and Blood.

Christ knew our hunger for himself. He knew that we would be walking around in the darkness of wars and miseries throughout this life. He knew that people would not all accept his commandment of love. He knew that we would be angry, and hurt and kill each other. In order to have someone walk over the waters as he did, the waters of all those human miseries, and to bring his peace there, he enters into the ones he has chosen as priests.

After his resurrection, Christ ascended to his Father, but he didn't want to leave us orphans—so he gave us the priesthood. In his immense love, Christ chose men in whom

he could walk, through whom he could forgive sins, men who could give us the sacrament of the most holy Eucharist, which he
said makes for life everlasting.

Christ wanted to give us someone in
whom we would see his resemblance as the
Lover, the Tender One, the Forgiving One,
the Servant. Someone who would do what he
did: wash the feet of humanity while, by a
simple gesture of hands and a few words, also
washing their souls. A priest brings to us
everything that Christ would bring to us.

In every priest Christ walks across the
width and breadth of our whole land; there
are no nooks and corners where he isn't present. In the eternal priesthood of Christ, new
priests will come forth. God the Father,
through Our Lady, in a manner of speaking,
will eternally beget them, again and again.

Being a priest encompasses heaven and
earth, time and eternity, men and God, saints
and sinners, the communion of saints and
the Mystical Body of Christ, life and death
and everything in between. For, as I wrote in
my poem, *What is a Priest?*:

A priest is a lover of God,
  a priest is a lover of men,
  a priest is a holy man
    because he walks before the face of the All-Holy.

A priest understands all things,
  a priest forgives all things,
  a priest encompasses all things.

The heart of a priest is pierced, like Christ's,
  with the lance of love.

The heart of a priest is open, like Christ's,
  for the whole world to walk through.

The heart of a priest is a vessel of compassion,
  the heart of a priest is a chalice of love,
  the heart of a priest is the trysting place
    of human and divine love.

A priest is a man whose goal is to be another Christ;
  a priest is man who lives to serve.

A priest is a man who has crucified himself
  so that he too may be lifted up
  and draw all things to Christ.

A priest is a man in love with God.

A priest is the gift of God to man
  and of man to God.

A priest is a symbol of the Word made flesh,
   a priest is the naked sword of God's justice,
   a priest is the hand of God's mercy,
   a priest is the reflection of God's love.

Nothing can be greater in this world than a priest,
   nothing but God himself.

2 | Teach us to pray

"One aspect of the priest's mission, and certainly by no means a secondary aspect, is that he is to be a 'teacher of prayer.' However, the priest will only be able to train others in this school of Jesus at prayer, if he himself has been trained in it and continues to receive its formation."

— *Pope John Paul II,*
Shepherds After My Own Heart, 47.

Dear seminarian, the first thing I want to speak of is prayer. Of all prayers, the Mass is best. Show us how to participate in it, what relation it has to our daily life, how it can permeate life and make every moment of it holy, giving us strength not only to withstand temptation but to be bold enough to bring our warm faith into a world cold with hate.

Please learn well the way of offering Mass; for every gesture you make, every word you say, has an infinite meaning, and will help us to understand and participate better, with greater recollection and deeper fervor. Make us aware that the rite of dismissal: "The Mass is ended, go in peace to love and serve the Lord," is a mandate we receive from the Lord to integrate this august sacrifice into our lives. Teach us how to live the Mass, how to plunge into that sea of fire and love and to merge our love with his until we ourselves become a fire that not only lights the path of our neighbors' feet to God, but makes their hearts burn with love of him.

Of course you will make it very clear that Communion is an integral part of the Mass. It is the Bread of Love, the Bread of Strength, on which alone we shall be able to fight the good fight and bring others to their loving Father, our Lord and God. The greatest prayer in the world is the Eucharist. I enter into contact with God, into communion with God, because he enters into me, and slowly I become like him—he who once became like me. This holy Banquet constantly forms us. It is an immense, extraordinary mystery of love.

The day is long, and we have to go into the thick of a world that has either forgotten God or learned to hate or ignore him. Many are our temptations. We need help. Living God's law of love is hell on our emotions and on our humanity. The only way we are able to follow the Lord's counsels is by prayer. By remembering that we are creatures and therefore totally dependent on God, who told us, "Without me you can do nothing." When we throw ourselves through prayer into his merciful heart he comes to help us to love as he wants us to love.

Please teach us that prayer must not cease because we are busy. Help us to make prayer a habit that will sustain us through times of feeling sluggish. Explain to us how we can pray on our way to work, to school, in the midst of a busy household day.

Tell us how to meditate on Scripture, especially the gospel, simply by thinking about and savoring Christ's words and actions. Urge us to do that regularly, so that we learn the mind of Christ. Introduce us to the spiritual nourishment in the Fathers of the Church and their teachings, for somewhere along the road of time we Catholics lost or mislaid the full heritage of the Spirit that was ours. Help restore it to us. Include the encyclicals of the popes.

Teach us to pray for faith, and to live out our faith, to be eager to share it. Teach us to be receptive to the Holy Spirit, to be alert to his word in our heart. Teach us how listening is an essential aspect of prayer.

Remind us that the Holy Trinity dwells in us. As Christ said, "My Father and I will come and abide in you." Remind us that God loves us, not because *we* are good, but because *he* is good. Tell us often of the goodness of God and his mercy, so that when the day is ended we may come to him without fears, with hearts truly filled with sorrow for our sins of omission and commission.

And don't forget that contemplative prayer belongs to us, too. We need this prayer of silence and love. Tell us about it in simple words, leaving out all the big vocabulary which love does not necessarily need. Make the prayer of contemplation easy for us, as easy as a mother contemplates her sleeping baby cradled in her arms—listening in an attentive silence.

Teach us that in order to make contact with God we must begin to smash the idols within ourselves that we worship, perhaps without fully realizing that we do so. For they are like stones tied to the kite of prayer.

We need priests who will teach us how to encounter God, how to know him, how to pray to him, how to love him. There are many ways of teaching people to know God, but the best way still is to show them. A priest's best teaching method is the measure in which he shows Christ through his life. Yes, dear seminarian, please get into the habit of prayer now. Make yourself ready to teach us to pray—so that we may learn to love God as he should be loved.

3 | Be seen;
be approachable

> "The faithful are often left to themselves for long periods, without sufficient pastoral support. As a result their growth as Christians suffers, not to mention their capacity to become better promoters of evangelization."
>
> — *Pope John Paul II,*
>   *Shepherds After My Own Heart, 7.*

Dear Seminarian, the need for bridging the gap between priests and lay people has been before us for years. The popes have described it better than I ever could, yet it bears repetition. This is what I have found to be the bridge, or at least its foundation.

The priest must *be seen.* By this I mean that he, like Christ, must constantly, simply, and naturally mingle with the people belonging to his parish. He must be seen walking through all its streets, wide and narrow, rich and poor; all its back alleys. He must be a familiar sight to Catholic and non-Catholic alike.

Have you ever stopped to consider what a blessing the presence of a priest is? If your soul is sensitive to God and the things of God, that blessing is almost palpable. The priest does not necessarily have to speak, he need only *be* in some place. That *being* of his will impart a blessing, bring God's grace, do so many almost miraculous things that are impossible to enumerate.

Let me tell you a little story about that. There was in the neighborhood of one of our Friendship Houses a most desolate street. It was desolate because God had literally been banished from it. At the time, every house on it was a Communist stronghold. Try as we might, we could not penetrate even the periphery of that tragic problem.

Loving priests as I do, it occurred to me that if I could induce one of them to walk daily through that street—just walk—that would do what nothing else seemed able to accomplish. I went to see a Jesuit. At first he said he could do "nothing of the sort." His work was teaching, he said, not converting a street. I reminded him that his doctor had prescribed an hour's walk daily for the sake of his health, and inquired if he needed any special permission as to which streets, which direction, to walk in. Having received the answer that he was free to walk wherever he pleased, I presented my plan to him. I begged him to walk daily through my desolate street. He agreed.

At first the unfamiliar sight of a priest drew jeers and curses from the dwellers of that street. Little by little the curses and jeers ceased. A year later, after having kept his promise and just silently walked through the desolate street, Father had to acknowledge that people were greeting him; mothers were begging prayers for their sick ones; children were running gleefully to meet him.

But we who knew that street, who watched it anxiously, we knew more. We knew that just the presence of a priest had brought untold benediction to the people on it. In the person of the priest it had brought Christ back to them; the mere 'sight' of Christ had brought them to their spiritual knees once again. The Communists lost that street, and on Sundays more and more families could be seen on their way back to church.

A priest who was serving in Brazil told me a similar story. His parish had been heavily Marxist and during his tenure he hadn't seen much growth in faith. When the time came for his transfer he suddenly remembered my telling the above story at the seminary where he had studied, and he asked for six months to try this thing out. He struggled to believe that he was an *alter Christus*, but he did believe it, and he walked the streets. He reported that his parish began to flourish, spiritually.

So when you become a priest, my friend, *be seen*. That's the thing I wanted to say first. Secondly, I beg you, *be approachable*, as Christ was approachable during his public ministry.

We live in an age that exemplifies the truth of Christ's beautiful parable about the lost sheep—we must leave the ninety-nine just to go after the one lost. Perhaps you will not consider me facetious if I say that it looks as if we have to leave the one just, in order to go after the ninety-nine lost!

The number of people falling away from the Church is tragically stupendous; the world is denying the very existence of God. This is not the day for theological and philosophical arguments, used in early post-Reformation times. Today it is a matter of bringing God back to people and people back to God. The priest must go to them, and not wait for them to come to him. This applies in regard to both Catholics and non-Catholics.

So it follows that the priest must be seen and be approachable, must be easily found, easy to talk to. We Catholics must shed our siege mentality. We must realize that to be on the defensive is pitiful. With the fullness of truth that is ours, we can and must be, proactive. Priests lead their people, being here, there, everywhere. Being, in fact, all things to all men—as was Christ, their supreme model.

A priest must talk our language. True, the hallmark of an educated man is his correct speech. But the language of the masses is not necessarily incorrect. It is simple, direct, at times rough or picturesque. Study it, my friend. Learn to speak it. Learn to present Christ and his teachings in words that all of us will understand. Imitate him. In his time, he spoke so that the little ones, the unlearned and the simple understood him as well as the others.

Yes, dear seminarian, after you have taught us how to pray, come and give us the benediction of your priestly presence. Be seen among us often. Be easy to approach. Speak our language, so that through you we may see Christ more clearly. We need to, because the darkness around us is intense.

4 | Set us on fire through your preaching

"The Spirit of the Lord is upon me because he has anointed me to preach good news to the poor."

— *Luke 4:18*

Dear seminarian, I know that today priests face a lot of resistance in proclaiming the practical applications of the gospel. Yet we need to hear them, spoken from the pulpit with all the authority and assurance that your holy priesthood gives you. We need them desperately, urgently, and constantly. At the risk of seeming monotonous, I repeat that your ministry is twofold: making the sacraments available to us, and teaching us, according to the mind of the Church, our mother.

One place is reserved very specifically in every Catholic church for this, your teaching ministry: the pulpit. In it, Sunday after Sunday and many times in between, you will stand to deliver to us your homily. It is then that you have all of us before you— the eager and the lukewarm, the learned and the ignorant, saints and sinners, rich and poor, married and single. This, then, is the 'acceptable' time and place for you to try to set us on fire with the love of God; to awaken us to the vast opportunities of serving God in our brothers and neighbors; in a word, to make us Catholics who not only 'belong' to the faith, but know it, understand it, love it—and hence live it.

Please don't be afraid of either our ignorance or our learning, or of our youth or mature age. The grace of God will come to us in torrents through your inspired words. Your life must make them alive for us—your life, your zeal, and your own love of God and us.

These days we need to be evangelizing people, although the fact remains that we are in a pre-evangelizing situation. There is a great mix up in the minds of many people—other things are mixed in with true faith. We've got to be very careful today, not to present a mish-mash. The priest has the job of rolling back the stone from where Christ is buried in people's minds— the stone of sin, fog, and confusion. Priests are called to bring him forth from this tomb.

Adapt the riches of the Church's spirituality to an ever-changing world situation. Channel the eternal unchangeable verities through yourself. Look for new words and new ways to express the eternally old yet eternally young teachings of God. Try to make pathways of understanding, leading to the encounter of men and women with God, new pathways over which the new generation may travel.

Please, dear friend, give us the fullness of truth, and the ramifications as they apply to us, even if it hurts, even if some of us are looking for priests who will preach what we want to hear. We may tend, foolishly, to seek preachers who distort the message of Jesus. Like St. Francis, you will need to become a 'fool for Christ.' It takes great courage, or rather great faith, to speak the full truth, but there is immense spiritual danger in not preaching it. Help us to face the Spirit of truth.

Jesus preached a whole truth: "Pick up your cross every day and follow me." "Love one another." "Forgive." "Serve one another." "Give to those who ask without counting the cost." "It will be harder for the rich man to enter heaven, than for a camel to pass through the eye of a needle." Christ was a revolutionary: he shook the world, and is still shaking it.

Help us to see that if the Good News of Jesus is to set us free, then we must open our hearts to a radical transformation. Please don't allow us to be tepid and live in the twilight zone of semi-truth. We need to be willing to put on the mind of Christ, instead of trying to conform his mind to ours.

I pray for your fortitude and your faith. Give us the fullness of the gospel and water down nothing of its austere yet joyous message. Be not afraid to ask much of us. Ask *all* of us. We are much more likely to answer your challenge if it is great, fiery, and full of love of God and us, than if you ask just a little of us, and so somehow leave us discontented and humiliated because we have not been found worthy of more.

Please prepare yourself to preach the truth clearly and with charity, for your words will be effective, not only in proportion to your knowledge, but in proportion to your *love.* Strange, perhaps, but we know about your love, almost instinctively. We sense your closeness to God. The great preachers, like St. Thomas of Aquinas, were not canonized for their eloquence and learnedness, but for their love of God. Teach us and lead us, through your words, and in your life. When we cannot see clearly anymore, the first person we need to encounter is a priest. Lead us away from the Babel Towers into the heart of the Lord.

5 | Form us to live out our prophetic role as baptized persons

"The person baptized belongs no longer to himself, but to him who died and rose for us. He is called to be subject to others, to serve them in the communion of the Church...."

— *Catechism of the Catholic Church, 1269.*

"Through baptism the faithful...are reborn as sons of God and must confess the faith they have received... By the sacrament of Confirmation the Holy Spirit endows them with special strength...and they are...obliged to spread the faith, both by word and deed, as true witnesses of Christ."

— *Lumen Gentium, 11.*

Dear seminarian, we need your help in order to recognize and live out our calling as baptized persons. The tremendous reality of the sacrament of baptism has not yet penetrated, invaded, or soaked into our bones, sinews, blood, mind, heart, soul. Most people today have not been exposed to the full meaning of the fantastic, incredible mystery of baptism and its fruits, nor to their responsibilities to live out the promises made by them, or in their name, when they were being baptized. It is a mystery that God wishes us to understand.

Since most Catholics are baptized as babies, something about this obligation to keep their baptismal promises—to renounce sin, to give themselves completely and without compromise to Christ—is lacking, because of not having received formation about this awesome sacrament. Oh, the ceremony is festive, and the child is all dressed up, but the very essence of it is often overlooked. Many people seem to consider it as nothing other than the ceremony—they get baptized and that's the end of it.

It seems that almost no one believes that the word 'sanctity' is really for them—or that it is composed of ordinary things that people do every day. The little things in our life may appear to be irrelevant and very matter of fact. But little things share in the mystery of Christ's Incarnation. They are part of that movement of the Spirit through which the whole world is being transformed. We need to know why our ordinary routine is sanctifying, and why we are doing it: to return the love of Someone who has loved us so tremendously. Then we become witnesses to God through our daily life.

Please teach us to live out our vocation as baptized laypersons, in all its immensity. Make us familiar with the full meaning of baptism, with the graces that come through it to help us live our daily life. If only we knew what baptism does to us! Because we are baptized we are empowered to preach the gospel, the good news of Christ. The one thing people need, above all, is to hear it preached by word and deed.

As you teach us about our baptismal responsibilities, encourage families to celebrate the baptismal days of all the members: father, mother and children. It is strange that birthdays are celebrated so gloriously, and baptismal days are omitted from celebration. For our baptism is the moment when we are really born in the Lord.

A candle can be lit and placed on the table so that, in this simple way, the family remembers that this person has become a light to the world—because that is what a baptized person is—and then remembers that their baptism into the death of Christ also means being given the life of Christ. It is a day to thank God for the gift of faith, and for his life in us.

Baptism is a sacrament to grow into; it is a key to our spiritual growth. We emerge from the baptismal waters into a new life, the new life that shone forth from Christ's tomb. In baptism we receive the graces to belong in a deep and abiding way to the Body of Christ. Because we are the Mystical Body of Christ, whatever we do, or don't do, has global repercussions. Nothing that you or I do is indifferent; it carries a message to the whole world. Teach us to see the grace of ordinary life, how Christ divinizes our ordinary, commonplace existence through his Incarnation.

We lay people have the vocation to restore the world to Christ through our ordinary human contacts in business or profession, in our family and neighborhood, witnessing to Christ and preaching the gospel by living it. It is essential to connect ordinary life—with its seemingly boring and repetitious details—with love, who is God. Please teach us to make that connection, give us that awareness.

Teach us to encounter God in the present moment. We meet God in every moment when we are doing his will in our life. We may be working or playing or resting; doing an unpleasant chore or enjoying a leisure moment. If what we are doing is in accord with God's will for us in that moment, then we encounter him; he is with us in a very real way, and what we are doing is sanctifying us.

God gives us faith in baptism, but we are expected to grow in faith—as we grow in size from child to adult—and to continuously mature in it. Our baptism makes us apostles of Christ and ambassadors of his Glad Tidings. We have to accept the responsibility to show Christ to our brother, to be involved with him and serve him. To be committed to Christ is to become a living gospel, so that others may learn from us. We have this fantastic power because, in our baptism, we died with Christ and we now live in Christ.

Our baptismal obligation involves an openness and attentiveness to the Holy Spirit, who we receive when we are immersed in, or sprinkled with, the waters of baptism. He remains in us, burning as a bonfire, burning as did the tongues of fire that descended upon the twelve Apostles. He will remind us of all that Christ taught while he walked the earth. Since we are a temple of the Holy Spirit, our thoughts, actions and desires are by right more his than our own.

Teach us what it means when we renew our baptismal vows during the Easter liturgy—that it means walking in the footsteps of Christ, without compromise. That it means changing the world through the witness of our lives. It takes courage to imitate Christ.

When we receive the sacrament of confirmation we receive strength from the Holy Spirit and become empowered to stand up for the truth, both in our words and through our lives. We can accept being jeered and laughed at, knowing that people do not easily accept the message of truth—whether in word or example—if it impinges on their doing what they want, when and how they want. But God is serious. In speaking the truth in a charitable way, we become a 'suffering servant' of the Lord. When God gives us an obligation, he gives us the means to carry it out. Courage is not lack of fear, but fear overcome by faith.

This is how we live out the prophetic vocation that comes with baptism. Whoever preaches the gospel, the commandments of love, by his life and by his words, is a prophet. We have to be prophets to one another.

Dear seminarian, please teach us to live this way, both through word and your example. Young people, especially, need this, because they have to face a lot of ridicule from their peers for living out their faith. The prophetic power is greatest when we fully accept insults, hardships and persecution, so that the power is more clearly seen to come from God, rather than from ourselves. But we need to remember that we can give God to people only if we have him, and we have him if only we pray.

6 | Overcome human weakness through the Mother of God

"Every aspect of priestly formation can be referred to Mary, the human being who has responded better than any other to God's call."

— *Pope John Paul II,*
   Shepherds After My Own Heart, 82.

Dear seminarian, you have said that you are concerned about giving scandal, and so you should, for you are set apart. Now is the time to review what it is that gives scandal to the 'little ones' in Christ, and in a special way to those who will become your greatest concern—the lost ones. True, you have also to think of the just who still are in the fold. But don't forget that the lost sheep does not seek the shepherd—that goes with being lost.

People identify you with the Church. Priests are so precious, that when one deviates an inch from the path of Jesus Christ, it hurts us all. People will be scandalized if you become hardened to the voice of

God's justice; if you are indifferent and complacent about the social ills of the world and of your flock, refusing to see their tragic plight and being unwilling to fight for the downtrodden.

You will give scandal if you become aloof and apart from them, selecting for your friends the rich and the powerful, upholding a social status quo that brings misery and sorrow. Should you consider that being a priest means to uphold a certain standard of living, then you will indeed scandalize people. Should you be unapproachable and have *Office Hours* on your parish door, this will turn many away from the Church. A priest must seek his sanctity, at least in part, in service.

Poverty and service somehow go together. In Christ these qualities blended; he was such an example of both. Nothing impresses people more than seeing the tangible likeness of men to Christ. Especially do they look for it in their priests. No matter what history may whisper to the contrary, no matter what they may tell you to your face, they hunger for a glimpse—in you—of the Man who had nowhere to lay his head. It helps them to carry their many burdens, to accept their own poverty, their frequently unsolvable economic problems. Ask the Mother of God to help you become dispossessed, as she herself did when she said yes to becoming God's mother.

The clear vision of the Christ-like role of the priest as servant of all has been dimmed through time, perhaps when the immense and holy dignity of his office became mixed in with earthly glory and power. This vision becomes blurred when a priest forgets that his mastery is one of humility, poverty, love and service; when he becomes associated with the ruling classes.

It is through this that ordinary people ceased to be at ease with priests, and that the gulf between clergy and lay people grew. It has become imperative to change these attitudes. Pope after pope urged the filling of this ever-growing gap. The gap will be filled by priests who express their priestly dignity through Christ-like humility, poverty, and availability in service.

As you are aware, today many priests are deeply wounded. Crucifixion and tombs are surrounding them under innumerable hidden guises. The 'de-sacralization' of priests is becoming a sport, in which even they sometimes participate, for example by referring to themselves as "President of the

Assembly." Many priests seem to have lost the idea of who they are; perhaps their true identity has been lost through lack of it being reflected back to them by their parishioners and Catholics in general.

A priest is human, he is a sinner, even as we lay people are. But the difference between him and me is that he is another Christ. You may try to get away from the fact that you are Christ, because it's too painful for you. But, dear friend, no amount of trying will make it possible to reduce this Christ, or to 'exorcise' him out of the priesthood. You have to know that you are another Christ, know it in your body, your sinews, your muscles, your hands, and your head. Ask the Lord to help you.

Priests suffer a deep loneliness, they are torn with the same needs as lay people, are rebellious at times because of the circumstances in which God places them. I understand why Jesus Christ chose Peter over John, to be pope. Peter is forever the weak one, having denied Christ three times. It struck me in the 'Resurrection' gospel how Christ asked Peter three times if he loved him, and then told him to feed his sheep, and that he was giving him the keys of the kingdom.

I often tell the story of my mother's response when I, as a girl of twelve, saw a drunken priest and came to tell her in horror. She calmly took me back to where I had found him, and together we got him to the rectory. Without a word she brought me home and then told me to find the baby's potty, wash it well, fill it with water, and bring it to her. She, in the meantime, cut some beautiful white lilies in the garden. She put the lilies in the potty and said to me, "Look, the lily doesn't change because it is in a potty. Christ in the priest never changes. That is why I made you kiss the hand of this drunken priest before we put him in the rectory."

A priest's true identity is powerfully affirmed through hearts that have faith in Christ's presence in him.

The essential elements in the on-going formation of a priest are Mary, the Mother of God, and prayer. Mary is your mother and can form you as a priest, because she formed her divine Son. Ask for the grace of childlikeness in your relationship with her. Look to her for clarification in every uncertainty. She has insights that are so profound, that if you give yourself up to Mary, you overcome every difficulty that comes your way. It's very important that as a young priest you hand yourself over to the Mother of God, and really listen, listen with your whole heart, to what she has to say. When you don't know what to do, ask her, and leave your mind open. She will come into it and you will know what to do.

The Mother of God loves priests, and future priests, with an incredible love. She cares for all priests, who are her sons, and carries them in her compassionate heart, and tells them, "Take this way" or "Go that way." As the mother of priests she is intensely interested in your every concern.

7 | Bring youth to Christ

"Young Christians, trained to have a mature missionary consciousness, must become apostles to their contemporaries... At the parish level a pastoral outreach should seek to engage them in dialogue and take advantage of favorable occasions for meetings on a larger scale..."

— *Pope John Paul II,*
   The Church in America, 48.

Dear Seminarian, I must speak to you of the hunger in youth, which you will have to fill tomorrow, when you step down from the altar of God, a priest forever. Prepare yourself now to fill their hungry hearts and souls, for many are seeking to be filled with the Bread of Life and the living waters of truth. In all parts of this vast continent, youth who have thirst are seeking. They are asking questions. We have not answered them in a way that is original, that is exciting—in the way that the gospel truly is exciting.

Youth are at a crossroads. The influence of materialism affects them. They need directions, guides, help. If they are left leaderless, they may, in our tragic modern desert of secularism, hedonism, and atheism, mistake the lying mirage for the real thing. Unless helped and guided, they may waste much of their zeal, courage, and fire, pursuing will-o'-the-wisps. They may even give up the search for the Holy Grail altogether. And that would be the greatest tragedy that could befall them and us.

Many are reckless in their search. Some are revolting against society, or are vacillating. There is a great interest among the young today in witches, in the affairs of the evil one. You will need to speak with them about it a little, for Satan has not disappeared. Explain to youth that there are certain things that they should never do, because the danger is tremendous for their soul. It is very important that you explain this, since many young people do not know what they are really looking for, and it is hard for them to know which is the right turn.

One of the greatest tragedies of today is loneliness. And if there is anybody lonely in this world, it's a teenager, because many are, at the moment, alienated from their fathers and mothers, and are roaming around not knowing what to do, where to go, what is happening, or what are the necessary priorities.

They need you, priest of tomorrow, who are young too, and whose vision is unimpaired by time and worldly prudence. They need you because we, the adults of this generation, have failed them. We have failed them and God, because our vision has been narrow, our charity cold, our zeal asleep; because we have asked too little of them; because we have given them stones instead of bread; because we have been prudent with the prudence of men, and not with the prudence of God.

We have often left them outside, looking in, because we have chosen—perhaps it called for too much effort on our part—to forget that youth has always been eager to lay down its life for an ideal. We must be done with indifference and complacency. Loss of a great many vocations is due to lack of interest in young souls who, one should be able to easily detect, are inclined toward them. Thanks be to God, today there are Catholic youth who are ready to follow Christ, even if they are ridiculed and persecuted for this.

What will you ask of them, my friend? Not to sin? To go to Mass on Sunday? Are they to go to God just on this? If only you show them the way, they can bring him sanctity—a positive, glorious, singing life—which, as it is lived, will by its very nature become a lamp to the feet of others. They themselves are called to leadership among their peers. Those who have thirst and are searching must pass on the Good News of Christ. They must bring others to him.

Young people like to touch reality. They also are looking for mystery. You yourself, by living the reality of the priesthood of Jesus Christ, will be one of the greatest mysteries! Help them to 'connect' with Jesus Christ, to pray to him. If you yourself are prayerful, they will know, and it will help them.

Make yourself ready, perhaps by getting some experience in youth work now. Please do not fail youth. If you do, the catacombs will engulf you, them, and all of us.

8 | Prepare for the long haul

"Stay awake, praying at all times for the strength to survive all that is going to happen..."

— *Luke 21:36*

Dear seminarian, we have concluded that people must be given *God*, in his fullness and beauty, through his commandments, his sacraments, especially Mass and the Holy Eucharist; through prayer and a life that is entirely Christ-centered. This must be given them through you and your parish-to-be, which to all is a channel of God's grace.

Fundamentally, it is through you that all these graces will flow into their hearts. It is you who will celebrate the Mass. It is through you that Christ will become the Bread and Wine of future saints. It is you who, in his name, will loose their souls from the slavery of sin. It is you who will make available all the sacraments except Ordination, which is conferred by the bishop, and matrimony, to which you are but a witness. Yet who is the bishop, and in what title does he glory most? That of priest— Father. For what can be greater than a priest of God?

How are you going to face this tremendous task? To accept this terrible and holy responsibility? Of course you will be ordained for it, and God will give you the graces needed for your ministry. He will do his part. He always does. But what about you? There is a saying: "A zealous priest, a fervent parish; a tepid priest, a cold parish." Which will you be?

Now, at the threshold of your ordination, you are aflame with zeal. The love of God consumes you. Your soul is hungry for God. Nothing is too hard for you. In him, through him, with him, for him, you are ready not only to die but also to live in his service—which at times is harder!

But tomorrow will come, dear friend, and with it the cold winds of everydayness, of loneliness, of monotony, of obstacles, of ingratitude, of misunderstandings, of ridicule, of hardship, of seeming failure and the need to begin all over again. What then?

Are you ready for all these and much more that cannot be told but must be lived, day by day, hour by hour, in the endless *Via Crucis* that is the path of all—and especially of his chosen ones—who are in love with Christ, who walked that way first? You will be ready if you remember that you must lead by example. To maintain the strength to do so, you must be close, ever so close, to your model, Christ.

Like him, be not concerned as to what you eat or how you sleep. In a word, be really poor in spirit and reality, so that you have to depend on God. Dispossession brings freedom. Be poor. Rely on Christ.

Prayer is your life. There you will find strength and faith, not only to persevere, but to become indeed another Christ, which you are meant to be. Your house may be next to your church. If your days are busy for him, there is always the night to pray before his very face. One hour before the Blessed Sacrament in each twenty-four, in the great silence of God, will help you over all the obstacles. However, you can pray in any place. Do not neglect prayer. Do not allow even the best and holiest works of mercy to become for you the heresy of good works, or to take you away from prayer.

The evangelists tell us that the Lord often arose long before daybreak and went out to a deserted place and prayed there. Because of the constant demands on your person, you will need regular periods of solitude and silence in order to remain available, interiorly and exteriorly, to people at other times. Our contemporary daily life is often filled with noise. Priests need to find a quiet place to get renewed and restored.

This solitude and silence may be difficult for you, because all kinds of thoughts will bombard your mind, like bullets. You need to stay in your 'desert' place and let them hit you. If you stay calm and let them hit you, they will suddenly cease and then you can begin to listen to God. It is very important that you cultivate your own 'journey inward,' so as to remain faithful in your most beautiful but difficult vocation.

9 | Keep the flame of love burning in your parish

"I have come to bring fire to the earth and how I wish it were blazing already!"

— *Luke 12:49*

Dear seminarian, you have been asking me for various ways and means that may help you, the future priest, to bring your flock closer to God. There is an old maxim in spiritual life that he who stands still, goes backward. If you are to keep the flame of love alive and burning in your parish, you will have to give your parishioners strong food for their souls, hearts, and minds, in order to help them to keep on growing in knowledge, love, and sanctity. Human nature is frail, and the darkness of original sin is still with us, not to mention the tragic fact that the Mystery of Iniquity is forever abroad.

A first step, of great importance, should be a personal survey of the social conditions of your parish. Assess its many shortcomings, its human needs, its weak spots.

Then make your plan according to your personal findings. Within your domain you may have the hungry and the destitute; the lame, the halt, and the blind, literally and figuratively; the lonely and shut-ins; the very old and very young, both at times abandoned. You will have restless, rudderless youth, and complacent middle age, losing its soul! And some who have lost their way entirely.

Teach your parishioners the social implications of the commandments and the gospel. Show how the Commandments of God are indeed commandments of love; that each word of them speaks to us of that love which is God. Explain that, in the final analysis, they are but signposts on the road of love, happiness, and peace—which is also the road to life everlasting.

Help us, your parishioners, to live the Beatitudes, the Sermon on the Mount. Teach us to see rightly who our neighbor is, and what our duties toward him are—in politics, economics, the social scene, labor, management. Open wide to us the sublime doctrine of the Mystical Body of Christ. We are all so intimately connected, so one; we are members of his body. We must become Christ-bearers, people who will bring him wherever we go: home, factory, business, marriage; birth, life, and death. Being Christ-centered changes our whole outlook.

In today's secular world, which worships wealth, power, status and, above all, comfort, how is the Church to teach the luminous gospel of Christ, which calls us to detachment, poverty of spirit, and even factual poverty? The only way she can do this is to become visibly poor herself in the lives of the men and women who *are* the Church—pope, bishops, priests, and lay people.

Many people in our society do not understand their obligation to Christ living in the poor. Help us to understand that what is beyond our necessity—food, shelter, clothing, the normal education of our children, and some provision for old age and ill health—belongs to the poor. The poor are God's ambassadors, the representatives of Christ—nay, Christ himself.

As the desire for simplicity and humility grows, the desire for possessions, wealth, worldly success and adulation begins to disappear. Then the great tranquility of God's order will descend through your parish, into people's souls and hearts. They will become a group of true Christians, of whom the world will have to say once more, "See how these Christians love one another."

The main channels of grace for this are the worship of God together and the reception of the sacraments, along with your homilies, which enlarge our spiritual horizons and motivate us to know and love God more. There are many secondary channels, too, through which grace will flow into your parishioners, including the corporal and spiritual works of mercy.

There are also many gracious and helpful 'para-liturgical' ways of living the liturgical year in Christ, and these are effective channels of grace. Family customs and traditions that celebrate feast days and liturgical seasons help to make the gospel permeate our whole life. The year begins with Advent and making ready for the birth of Christ. Encourage families to make and use an Advent wreathe, lighting one of its four candles during supper on the first week, two on the second week, and so on.

Lent will follow, a preparation for the final act of our redemption, the crucifixion, and the glories of the resurrection. There are so many customs that can enhance the understanding of the Lenten and Paschal seasons. The spiced 'hot-cross buns' for Good Friday carry the symbolism of the myrrh and other aromatics used in the burial of Christ. Easter eggs may be decorated with liturgical symbols, and Paschal bread blessed. Encourage 'alms of the heart,' such as tenderness, forgiveness, a smile and a kind word; and 'alms of service' to others.

Like a flower slowly opening in all its beauty, para-liturgical costumes and traditions will bring old and new ways into your parish life. Young love may have its engagement blessed. New mothers may be blessed. Houses, rooms, and apartments, too, may be blessed by you, to the joy of their occupants. Since God imparts to a priest his power to bless, I am a little astonished that people do not ask the blessing of the priest when he comes to their home. It is wonderful to be blessed, for it is Christ who blesses through the priest, and his blessing is very powerful, and warm. Blessings are one thing that the devil is certainly afraid of.

Encourage praying the rosary as part of daily life for families, and the use of holy pictures, crucifixes, and holy water in your parishioners' homes. Lauds and Vespers can become part of parish life.

Life is a journey in search of the 'full' Christ within us—a *journey inward* that should begin early, seeking Christ within the depths of our souls in order to know him better, love him more, and worship him with an ever greater understanding of who it is we are worshiping. This growing knowledge and love will transform us into fires of zeal and service: zeal for our Father's house and our neighbor's salvation.

10 | Prepare to give us spiritual direction

"It is necessary to rediscover the great tradition of personal spiritual guidance, which has always brought great and precious fruits to the Church's life…. Priests, for their part, should be the first to devote time and energies to this work…"

— *Pope John Paul II,*
  Shepherds After My Own Heart, 40.

Dear seminarian, your very presence, as I've said, brings grace and benediction. When you fulfill the duties of your ministry, for which you will soon be ordained, grace flows through you to us. The very thought of its immensity fills my heart with overwhelming gratitude to God. What, besides the sacraments, can bring these graces so abundantly to us, who have to struggle to live out our faith? Why, your teaching. And what more effective way is there to teach than by directing a soul to God? This, too, can become part of your ministry of teaching. Spiritual direction is a personalized form of our spiritual formation.

For how can we walk the 'royal road' to Christ without a guide, especially in these bewildering days? The road to God is narrow, steep and hard, and surrounded by pitfalls and precipices. One walks at times in complete darkness, or in a sort of blurred twilight in which the signposts, standing at its many crossroads, are well nigh unreadable.

Nor must we forget that the evil one is powerful and ever present. How can we distinguish and fight Satan, the master of disguises, who can mix truth with lies so skillfully, who often tries to confuse the signposts to God, unless you stand by to guide and instruct us, to direct our souls and steps? Spiritual direction is at the heart of all the graces given in Ordination. You will be ordained to lead to Christ all those your life touches, to bring him saints.

I raise my tiny, humble voice and state with all the simplicity of a soul filled with love, respect and utter faith, that what we need in these contemporary times is spiritual direction—priests who can give it to individuals on a deep personal level. Spiritual direction seeks to lead the unique, individual person to the perfection desired by God, and for which he has given this person certain talents and graces. Without spiritual guidance individuals normally cannot develop their full spiritual and active potential.

Yet I know, dear friend, that you are somewhat afraid of this part of your ministry. Perhaps you do not feel adequately prepared. I grant that special training may be needed in order to give spiritual direction according to the mind of God and his Church, and the needs of individual persons. I understand the science and art of spiritual direction to be an application of both ascetical and mystical theology. I pray that some day this will form part of all seminary training. It is important that you yourself continue to have spiritual direction. People seek your holiness to help their holiness on its way.

You can prepare for this sacred task by study, reading, and prayer. Then, when you are a priest of God and some eager soul asks you in all simplicity, as a child of God and his Church, to be their spiritual director and guide on the road to sanctity, why not launch into the deep, and try? Continue to study, pray, and read while launching, and profit by your mistakes.

There is a tendency toward mediocrity at every phase in the development of our spiritual life. We are immensely grateful for spiritual directors who do not let us become complacent in the 'peace' of an established routine, who urge us to die to our selfishness and to grow in wholehearted love of God. To teach souls to surrender is to teach them to love. Surrender means selflessness. So don't just give us TLC; sometimes you will need to tell us to 'get up and go,' in order to follow Christ more closely.

One of the first challenges that will confront you in giving spiritual direction is the dire need to distinguish emotional problems from spirituality. Be careful not to mix spiritual direction with psychological counseling. Be alert so as not to be manipulated, and to see the layers of masks that many of us are prone to use. Fifty years of working in the apostolate have slowly, painfully shown me a glimpse of things I originally didn't suspect were there. It is increasingly important for priests to recognize the symptoms of neurosis and to be able to recommend competent outside help for same, if needed.

You have to be alert, too, so as not to allow your own personality to impinge on spiritual direction. St. John of the Cross said, "It is the Holy Spirit who directs, so I have to disappear." Try to allow yourself to be a vehicle of the Holy Spirit. This is what people are seeking, not your great knowledge. A spiritual director needs to be detached from everything but God. St. John of the Cross describes a spiritual director as a man who sits back, as it were, and watches the workings of the Holy Spirit in the heart and soul of another. Never interjecting himself, he guides each person according to the Wind and the Fire that he sees in them.

He must cleanse himself of many things because he is to listen to the works of the Holy Spirit, and these are heard in silence and prayer. A priest who gives spiritual direction has to work at it, in constant prayer, so as to be detached from everybody, and so as not to feed his own ego through his directing. You have to die to self, in giving spiritual direction.

I might mention that some of you have asked how you could best help us laypersons to take on evangelization, as the popes have been urgently calling us to do. One answer comes to me immediately: it is this *direction of souls.* We all know that grace comes to people through others. Thus God ordained it in his infinite wisdom, and it comes in a very special manner through his priests. When all is said and done, the priest, through the sacrament of Ordination, has the power from above to deal with questions of faith and morals—of which finding one's true vocation in life, for example, is an integral part. Vocations would flourish if youth could get individual, personal spiritual direction. Thus this 'pearl of great price' would not be lost.

Future shepherd of our souls, on the day of your ordination you receive powers beyond imagining. You become a vessel of the Almighty. You have the gift of communicating God's truth to people. Evil spirits fear and obey your words. Open your mouth and the Lord will speak through you. You may feel hesitant, but your guidance will help to transform us into saints. Teach us how to love as God desires.

I pray much for you, our future priests, for it is you who will have to be our guides on the long, strenuous, and even frightening journey inward that we all need to make—the journey to our final end, so that we reach heaven in a blaze of glory and love, as we are meant to. Please don't neglect your own need for spiritual direction. Then take on our souls, leading them to God.

11 | Encourage the new lay movements and 'ecclesial communities'

> "There is a great need for alive Christian communities! The new ecclesial communities are the... providential response given by the Holy Spirit to the critical challenge at the turn of the millennium."
>
> — *Pope John Paul II, May 30th, 1998.*

> "The originality of the new communities often consists in the fact that they are composed of mixed groups of men and women, of clerics and lay persons, of married couples and celibates..."
>
> — *Pope John Paul II, Consecrated Life, 62.*

Dear seminarian, I would like to talk with you now about certain apostolic laypersons in whom the Holy Spirit—the Spirit of wisdom, the giver of vocations—has dropped his all-consuming fire of love and bade to arise and to till a portion of the Lord's vineyard. To begin with a brief historical perspective: the call to the "lay apostolate" became especially noticeable after

1925, when one of the first letters on what was then known as "Catholic Action" came from the Pope. True, it was addressed to bishops, but it seems that the Holy Spirit made it his business to spread the suggestions to the souls of lay people.

For, from the four corners of the earth arose men and women whose names became familiar in the early lay apostolates. Frank Duff of Ireland and the *Legion of Mary*. Dorothy Day of the *Catholic Worker*. The ladies of the *Grail* in Holland. Mounier of *L'Esprit* in Paris. Foulliot and the *Companions of St. Francis*, in the same city. The *Young Christian Workers* movement took on new life in those days, as did many others too numerous to mention here. They surmounted indifference and hatred, ignorance and poverty, which close people's minds to the light of God's truth. They set about changing darkness to light, sin to grace.

Were you to talk to the people who were involved in these early lay movements* and ask what was their heaviest cross, their bitter-

---

* Contemporary ecclesial communities include: Focolare, the Beatitudes, Madonna House, Neo-Catechumenal Way, Marie-Jeunesse, Emmanuel, Solitude Myriam, Shalom, and numerous others. See the appendix for a description.

est cup and gravest temptation, they would tell you that it was the fear and suspicion they met in the majority of the clergy. A fear and suspicion of the very things that made them apostles in the market place: enthusiasm for God and the things of God, burning zeal for their Father's house, all their apostolic endeavors.

Because they dared to be different, tried desperately to become complete Catholics, to live the gospel of Christ, to restore the world to him, to bind the numerous deep wounds of the Mystical Body, without red tape and in an original manner, many of these lay apostles were suspected, questioned, discredited, and even persecuted by those from whom they expected their greatest support.

The growth of the lay apostolate depends on cooperation between lay people and clergy. This perforce must embrace a mutual dialogue. Lay apostles want your understanding, sympathy and guidance in the workings of their apostolate. They want to restore the world to Christ, including bringing to you those who have lost their way—with whom, incidentally, they are in closer contact through daily life than you can be. Their fundamental desire is to preach the Gospel by living it to the full, and integrating into daily life all its shining principles and commands.

New Christian communities of laymen, women, and priests are being called into existence by the Holy Spirit, who forms them to become a fire burning in our midst, a fire whose sparks kindle the earth. God calls the members to open their hearts to others—to all their fears and angers and unshed tears. We carry another's crosses because Christ carried ours.

I might mention that in these new communities the relations between priest and lay members are especially close, and the example given by the priests is formative. For the priest, the new communities can provide a laboratory of humility, approachability, poverty and simplicity, which inevitably lead to a burning desire to serve and not to be served. Both lay members and priests must learn in the same school of love.

The role of Christians is changing. This does not mean that we abandon the corporal works of mercy, for the poor will remain with us always. But our contemporary accent will be to show that Christ is alive, that the Holy Spirit is with us in a continual Pentecost. This can only be shown by a growth of love among us so that all the neo-pagans and atheists of today will be compelled to say, "See how these Christians love one another." This is the witnessing that all are called to today, but especially those in communities, whether traditional religious orders, or the new ecclesial communities.

How desperately people all over the world need communities of love, as in the early Christian times, where they can come in order to be healed, to renew their shaken faith, to find not only love but understanding, and to rest in. Members of these new communities serve the broader community, for love always spills itself in service.

True, their burning zeal may make your life 'uncomfortable,' or add new burdens or works to your future ministry; their zeal may lead you, by sheer weight of example, into new spiritual paths that you are scarcely ready to travel! But the Lord God himself definitely wants these lay movements and new communities to take root in our dangerous century. Directives regarding them come, with warm expression, from the very heart of Christendom, the Holy Father.

Appendices

Ecclesial communities

by Mark Schlingerman,
director-general of lay men,
Madonna House Apostolate

One aspect of discernment and vocation is that it is the call of one who loves us. God finds ever-new ways to call us, and this is about one of the new ways God calls us to himself.

Over the centuries he has done this in different ways. For example, after the martyrs in the early years of the Church, came monasticism. Out of monasticism as a way of life, came the mendicants: monks on the road, so to speak. From that, missionaries; the Holy Spirit sent men and women off into the world, individually.

At this present point in the history of the Church, the Holy Spirit has introduced ecclesial communities. (I would mention here that after the death of our foundress, Catherine Doherty—which coincided with a change in canon law—the directors-general of our Madonna House community went to Rome to find out exactly where we fit in the Church's thought. They were told that we were part of a movement of the Holy Spirit that was taking place, but that it was too early to give that movement any kind of definition. This was in 1989.)

In 1998 the Pope, at a meeting of some other of these communities at St. Peter's, on Pentecost, began to talk about what are now called new "ecclesial movements and communities":

> Today a new stage is unfolding before you, that of ecclesial maturity. There is a great need today for mature Christian personalities, conscious of their baptismal identity; of their vocation and mission in the Church and in the world. There is great need for living Christian communities.
>
> And here are the movements and the new ecclesial communities! They are the response given by the Holy Spirit to this critical challenge at the end of the millennium. You are this providential response! Thanks to this powerful ecclesial experience, wonderful Christian families have come into being, which are open to life— true domestic churches.

What follows is a brief glance at what I think ecclesial communities look like. The term 'ecclesial' is a rather large grouping, but I've taken several traits, which they seem to share in common.

First, they share a history. The ecclesial communities don't just come out of nowhere; that doesn't happen. They have a history, coming out of the *lay* apostolate. In the late 1800's the popes started issuing encyclicals, in particular, *Rerum Novarum*, which brought forward lay people in the Church. After World War I, Pius X talked about "restoring all things in Christ"; that mission was primarily given over to lay people, by virtue of the call received through our baptism.

Our own foundress, Catherine, sensed this in the 1930's, when the lay apostolate was just beginning to take shape. She said to a little group of her followers in Toronto, who made their commitment by taking simple Promises at St. Michael's Cathedral, in 1934:

> The lay apostolate is the coming event of the Church. More and more it will be at the forefront. Filled with the spirit of Christ, it will go and conquer the world. O Lord, give me a small share of that work—small and simple. But allow me to participate in it out of love for Thee and my neighbor.

We will find that many of the new communities have origins in the lay apostolates.

Next, they group together—and this was new—men and women in the same community and, in some cases, both single people and married couples, all within one community.

They also involve laity and clergy within the same community.

The pope speaks of this, of men and women, single and married, lay people together with clergy:

> One of the gifts of the Spirit in our times is undoubtedly the flourishing of the ecclesial communities, which ever since the beginning of my pontificate I have continued to point out as a source of hope for the Church, and for man. They are a sign of the *freedom of forms*, in which one Church is realized.

They bring together all the different basic vocations within the Church: marriage, celibate life, religious life, and the priesthood.

Another thing that characterizes these new ecclesial communities is that usually they are anchored in some kind of direct service to the poor, and have an understanding that the poor one is also my brother or sister next to me in the community.

Then, almost all of them are strongly Marian in character. They also usually speak, in their literature, about the life of Nazareth. The 30 hidden years of Christ's life are a model for community life.

And many of them have, as part of their spirituality, the work of accompanying the forsaken Christ, or being with Christ on Calvary. They bring us to an awareness of the neglect of Christ at this time in our history.

To sum up what I see as the overarching charism, the center, of these ecclesial communities: it is that they present to those who enter into them, Church. The Church, not primarily a *work* of the Church (such as teaching, hospitals, missions, or whatever). Rather a wholeness of Church, which involves relationships. You enter into relationships, relationships between the various vocations within the Church itself: clergy, laity, men, women, married, single. In the pope's words, they are the true domestic Church. That's what people 'walk into,' for the most part.

This desire for unity and trust among vocations, among the movements and communities themselves, (and between the Christian East and West,) is indeed central to the spirit of the new movements and ecclesial communities. They wish to reflect the words of John's gospel:

> May they be so completely one that the world will realize that it was you who sent me. (John 18:23)

As one commentator says:

> The intention of these ecclesial communities is that of presenting the communion between various vocations within the Church herself.

This is important. We know that in the situation in the Church today, not only in the United States but everywhere else, various problems have shown that the laity and the clergy don't necessarily trust one another. I'm sure these ecclesial communities are brought by the Holy Spirit, in part, to show that laity and clergy can learn to trust one another, to be one within the Church.

Now I want to look at one particular community, the one that I know best, Madonna House, in order to illustrate these traits.

Looking at our early history, certainly Catherine was an essential part of the lay apostolate, and even a pioneer in it, through her founding of Friendship Houses, which served the poor, in Toronto in the 1930's, and later in Harlem, New York—where the work focused on interracial justice.

Regarding men and women being in one community, Madonna House was one of the first groups to have that. From the very first group who came to work with Catherine in Toronto and made their commitment in 1934, Catherine's apostolate has been composed of men and women. We live under one constitution.

When Catherine went to Rome in 1951, to the first Lay Congress there, Cardinal Montini, who later became Pope Paul VI, asked her to continue this work of having men and women in the one community. Catherine had asked if this was wise, for it was a bit of a scandal at that time. He replied to her: *Madame must trust the Holy Spirit*. Pope Pius XII later ratified to Catherine that Madonna House should continue receiving both men and women as members of the same community, and we have done that. Trust in the Holy Spirit is essential.

The next point is that laity and clergy live within the same community. Priests came to join Madonna House in the 1950's; we had been a lay community up to that point. Later, in the 1960's, Catherine spoke with great wonderment at the mystery and gift of priests having come to join the fledgling community:

> The priests have been brought to a little flock especially selected and brought into being by God himself, a flock that is also the people of God. By the priests' coming to Madonna House, with the approval of the bishop, Madonna House now becomes a complete little Church: bishop, priests, people of God. Yet this little Church is not a parish, or a religious order. It is a little Church on pilgrimage, on a special pilgrimage—for it both has, and has not, a permanent physical abode. It goes where it is needed.

That's a marvelous reflection of who we are, of the little Church that the pope talks about, the domestic Church. The Church on pilgrimage. A community based on the original community, which is the Holy Trinity. That reality of relationships which people enter when they come into a community, relationships taking their origins in the Holy Trinity.

We are certainly anchored in the poor. Apart from the fact that most of us who are attracted to this community tend to be poor in some way or other, our first house was a hostel, a place of welcome in the Yukon, for people in need of shelter, food and clothing. Our other early houses, which we have continued, include soup kitchens for men and women on the street, and various kinds of neighborhood work. We continue to see in our work with the poor— our *collaboration* with the poor: hospitality and friendships, feeding and clothing—an anchor to our life, and a protection in our vocation.

We're certainly Marian. The presence of Our Lady of Combermere as our main helper and guide is extremely important for this family. Catherine and Fr. John Callahan, the first priest member, understood, early on, that Madonna House was "a gift of Our Lord to his Mother." As such, it is she who brings each person here. She is really the director of Madonna House.

And we always speak about Nazareth and the hidden life, about doing little things well for the love of God, about sanctity in ordinary life. God comes to us in the duty of the moment. Part of that duty of the moment is to allow the Holy Spirit to show us the underlying unity we have with one another by virtue of our common baptism. This unity of mind and heart we call *sobornost*, a Russian word containing that meaning. It expresses how we desire to live with one another.

Finally, one of the phrases that Catherine uses in speaking of our work of living with each other, of praying and witnessing, is that we are called to "assuage the loneliness of Christ," in the person that we meet and attend to.

So, we seem to be part of that set of factors that shape ecclesial communities. Catherine Doherty was one of the first to have the intuition that the lay apostolate was a thing of the future, and then to allow the Holy Spirit to fashion this community of Madonna House so that it truly became, and could be called one of the earliest of the ecclesial communities within the Church. We don't call ourselves that, but we seem to be just that.

Fr. Bob Wild, the postulator in Catherine's cause for canonization, sees in her one of the forerunners of this movement that the Holy Spirit is working within the Church now. There seems to be truth in that. She saw this happening, way before it became a reality. Her voluminous writings can be a real guide to the work that the Holy Spirit is doing in fashioning these communities.

So ecclesial communities are one of the ways that God calls us to himself. He is using those who come to join this community, both for service to the poor and for calling others into the Church. It is something that is really worth looking at, for those who are searching for a vocation and listening to what the Holy Spirit is saying.

From a teaching given by Mark Schlingerman as part of the 2003 Madonna House 'Summer Program,' week IV, which had as its focus *Hearing God's Call: Discernment & Vocation.*

A program for men discerning a call to priesthood

Madonna House Apostolate

Under the inspiration of Catherine Doherty, and in response to the Vatican proposal that men preparing for the priesthood undergo a time of spiritual formation before beginning studies in the seminary, Madonna House has, since 1980, offered a program of spiritual formation for men interested in the priesthood.

We seek to give you, the participant, a good experience of prayer, work, silence, daily liturgy, spiritual direction, simplicity of life, and service to one another. The program is an introduction to the fundamentals of the spiritual life.

The goal is that you develop not only knowledge of what constitutes the spiritual life, but also a habit of living it, so that when you get to the seminary you have that basic formation "under your belt," so to speak, and can then take on the intellectual work at the seminary. The program also is effective in the process of discerning a vocation to priesthood.

If you are interested, please contact us:

Postal address:

Director, Spiritual Formation
Madonna House Apostolate
2888 Dafoe Rd, RR 2
Combermere, ON K0J 1L0
Canada

E-mail: registrar@madonnahouse.org
Web site: www.madonnahouse.org

About the author

Catherine de Hueck Doherty

Born in Russia in 1896 of wealthy Orthodox parents, Catherine Doherty barely escaped death while fleeing the Communist Revolution. Before settling in Canada, she was received into the Catholic Church; she eventually became a lecturer, travelling a circuit that took her all across North America. Catherine established Friendship Houses that served the poor, first in Toronto and later in Harlem, where the focus of her work was interracial justice. In 1947 she and her husband Eddie Doherty moved to Combermere in rural Ontario, where her example of radical gospel living became a magnet for men and women in search of a way to live their faith. Soon the community of Madonna House was born—an open family of lay men, lay women, and priests.

In his thesis, *Staritsa: The Spiritual Maternity of Catherine de Hueck Doherty*, Fr. Don Guglielmi writes:

Catherine was a spiritual mother for the 20th century. She articulated an ancient tradition and made it intelligible for the modern age. Catherine recognized that she was living in an era of de-Christianization characterized by hedonism, materialism, and a narcissistic culture, and understood its cause—a turning away from God. She offered an antidote with the Little Mandate, her particular vision of living the Gospel without compromise. This was her 'word' to the spiritually darkened world of the 20th century, a word that has perennial value because it is rooted in the Gospel of Jesus Christ.

One of Catherine's most unique contributions was her spiritual motherhood to priests. Catherine called this her 'second vocation': 'My first love is God, and my second love is priests.' God gave Catherine a tremendous capacity to love priests, to spiritually nurture them, and to offer her life as a victim-soul for their salvation. She recognized that they, too, had become spiritual casualties upon the landscape of a secular culture.

In her talks, writings and correspondence with priests Catherine addressed various issues and themes that pertain to priestly life and formation, but her starting point was always priestly identity—the priest extends the incarnation of Christ in history; he is an icon of Christ, or 'another Christ.' She sought to nurture in priests an awareness that their vocation is divine and supernatural, and an intimacy with Jesus Christ. Her contribution to them cannot be underestimated; Catherine's spiritual motherhood to priests was a factor in saving a number of vocations, and leading others to deeper holiness.

Catherine Doherty died in 1985, and the cause for her canonization is in process; she is officially recognized as a 'Servant of God.' More information about her life, works, and cause for canonization can be found at:

www.catherinedoherty.org

The Little Mandate

Words which Catherine Doherty believed she received from the Holy Spirit, and which guided her life.

Arise—go! Sell all you possess. Give it directly, personally to the poor. Take up my cross (their cross) and follow me... going to the poor... being poor... being one with them... one with me.

Little—be always little! Be simple... poor... childlike.

Preach the gospel with your life, without compromise! Listen to the Spirit, he will lead you.

Do little things exceedingly well for love of me.

Love... love... love... never counting the cost.

Go into the marketplace and stay with me. Pray, fast... pray always... fast. Be hidden. Be a light to your neighbour's feet. Go without fears into the depth of men's hearts. I shall be with you.

Pray always. I will be your rest.

Madonna House Publications
Combermere • Ontario • Canada

"Lord, give bread to the hungry, and hunger for you to those who have bread," was a favourite prayer of our foundress, Catherine Doherty. At Madonna House Publications, we strive to satisfy the spiritual hunger for God in our modern world with the timeless words of the Gospel message.

Faithful to the teachings of the Catholic Church and its magisterium, Madonna House Publications is a non-profit apostolate dedicated to publishing high quality and easily accessible books, audiobooks, videos and music. We pray our publications will awaken and deepen in our readers an experience of Jesus' love in the most simple and ordinary facets of everyday life.

Your generosity can help Madonna House Publications provide the poor around the world with editions of important spiritual works containing the enduring wisdom of the Gospel message. If you would like to help, please send your contribution to the address below. We also welcome your questions and comments. May God bless you for your participation in this apostolate.

Madonna House Publications
2888 Dafoe Rd, RR 2
Combermere ON   K0J 1L0
Canada

Internet: www.madonnahouse.org/publications

E-mail: publications@madonnahouse.org

Telephone: (613) 756-3728